A Taste of L
Delectable Treat
Exotic Floral I

Gloria Hander Lyons

Blue Sage Press

A Taste of Lavender
Delectable Treats with an Exotic Floral Flavor

Inquires should be addressed to:
Blue Sage Press
48 Borondo Pines
La Marque, TX 77568
www.BlueSagePress.com

ISBN: 978-0-9790618-6-8

Library of Congress Control Number: 2007907005

First Edition: October, 2007

Printed in the United States of America

Table of Contents

Lavender is a beautiful, fragrant and tasty herb that has a wide range of culinary uses.

Delight your family and dinner guests by adding the deliciously distinctive flavor of lavender to your cooking.

Introduction

A Taste of Lavender

Lavender is more commonly known for its use in bath and beauty products, as well as in aromatherapy, for its pleasant fragrance and soothing qualities. It is also a popular choice for gardeners in America because of its beautiful, fragrant, purple flowers. But French chefs have been using lavender for centuries to add its sweet, floral flavor to their cuisine.

Thankfully, this tasty herb has finally found its way into the spice racks in American kitchens. Lavender can add a unique, exotic flavor to a wide variety of recipes, ranging from beverages to desserts to casseroles.

A member of the mint family, it tastes very similar to rosemary, with a hint of citrus. You can substitute lavender for rosemary in many recipes and the flowers (also called buds) can be used either fresh or dried.

The secret to cooking with lavender is: a little goes a long way. Start with a small amount and add more to taste. Adding too much lavender to your recipe will make it very pungent and bitter tasting. Dried lavender has a stronger flavor than fresh, so use one third the amount.

NOTE: Make sure the lavender you use for cooking has not been sprayed with any pesticides. It should be labeled "FOR CULINARY USE".

English Lavender (lavendula angustifolia) has the sweetest fragrance of all the lavenders, and is the one most commonly used in cooking.

Lavender blends well with any fruit, especially citrus. The citrus flavor of lavender enhances any recipe made with lemon. You can add extra zip to lemonade, pound cake or lemon chicken with this tangy herb.

The French used lavender to create an herbal blend called Herbs de Provence, which usually includes basil, oregano, sage and rosemary. You can find it in most supermarkets or make your own using the recipe on page 37.

If you don't plan to grow your own lavender, you can order dried lavender buds online. See the ordering information in the index.

Whether you're crafting soothing bath and body products or cooking a tasty treat, lavender is a welcome and versatile herb to have on hand.

Experiment with lavender in some of your own favorite recipes in addition to the ones included in this book. Lavender will add a unique flavor to your cooking.

Contraindications and Safety: It is recommended that lavender be avoided if you are pregnant or nursing. Also, it should not to be used with preparations containing iron and/or iodine. If you are taking prescription medications, check with your physician about possible contraindications for any herb.

Lavender Recipes

Cooking with lavender is no great mystery. You can add dried culinary lavender to many of your favorite recipes, from cookies to soup to meatloaf—no special recipe is required.

There are two methods for introducing the flavor of lavender into your food: by adding the dried buds directly to your dish or by infusing liquids with the lavender before adding them to the other ingredients. A few guidelines are described below:

Lavender Infusion

To infuse the flavor of lavender into your recipes, first steep the buds in water, milk, cream or sugar syrups before adding them to your food.

Measure one tablespoon of dried lavender buds for each cup of hot liquid (usually boiling water or warmed milk). Steep for 10-15 minutes and then strain the liquid. You can also steep the buds in cold milk or cream for 3-4 hours to infuse the flavor without warming the liquid.

Lavender water infusion can be used to flavor lemonade, iced tea and sorbets. Lavender milk or cream infusion can be used to make ice cream, cheese cake, scones or cakes.

Tips for Adding Dried Lavender to Recipes

- Use dried culinary lavender as you would any other dried herb in casseroles, soups or stews. It's best to grind the dried flower buds first in a clean coffee grinder then stir them into the dish.

- For meat, fish or poultry, blend 1 part ground, dried culinary lavender and 2 parts garlic powder (or a mixture of garlic powder and onion powder), plus salt and pepper to taste. Rub on the meat before roasting or grilling.

- Add 2 teaspoons of ground, dried culinary lavender to any bread, cake or cookie mix or recipe, including yeast breads, layer cakes, pound cakes and sugar cookies. Mix and bake as directed.

Helpful Hint: Grind several tablespoons of dried culinary lavender buds in a clean coffee grinder and store in an airtight container so you will have it on hand whenever you need it.

Impress your family and guests by adding the unique flavor of lavender to your favorite recipes. Just remember, it has a strong flavor, so use it sparingly. You will be pleasantly surprised with the results.

Beverages

Lavender Tea

Steep 1 teaspoon of dried culinary lavender buds in one cup of boiling water for three to five minutes. Strain the tea into a cup. Sweeten with honey or sugar if desired and serve with lemon. Lavender tea is good for insomnia or when you want to relax.

Relaxing Lavender & Herb Tea

1 tablespoon dried culinary lavender buds
1 tablespoon dried rosemary leaves
1 tablespoon dried mint leaves
1 tablespoon dried chamomile flowers
1/2 teaspoon whole cloves

Blend all the herbs and spices together and store in an airtight container. To prepare, place 1 to 1-1/2 teaspoons of tea mixture per cup of water into a warmed teapot. Pour boiling water over the herbs and steep for 5 minutes. Strain into cups. Serve with honey or sugar and lemon.

Lavender & Green Tea

1 tablespoon dried culinary lavender buds
1 tablespoon green tea leaves

Blend lavender and tea together and store in an airtight container.

To prepare, place 1 teaspoon of tea mixture per cup of water into a warmed teapot. Pour boiling water over the herbs and steep for 5 minutes. Strain into cups.

Sweeten with honey or sugar if desired.

Lavender & Lace Tea

1/2 teaspoon dried culinary
    lavender buds
1 teaspoon dried rose petals
    (labeled for culinary use)
2 tablespoons black tea leaves

Blend ingredients together and store in an airtight container.

This recipe makes one six-cup pot of tea. Place tea mixture into a warmed teapot. Add six cups of boiling water and steep for 3 to 5 minutes. Strain into cups.

Sweeten with honey or sugar if desired.

Packets of Lavender & Lace Tea make nice favors for tea parties when bundled in a pretty lace handkerchief and tied with satin ribbon. Be sure to attach the instructions for preparing the tea.

Lavender Lemonade

6 cups water (divided)
1-3/4 cups sugar
2 tablespoons dried culinary lavender buds
1 teaspoon grated lemon zest
1 cup fresh squeezed lemon juice

Combine 2 cups of the water, sugar, lavender and lemon zest in a large sauce pan. Bring to a boil.

Reduce heat and simmer, stirring frequently until sugar dissolves. Remove from heat and let syrup steep for 10 minutes. Strain syrup and discard lavender.

In a large pitcher, combine lavender syrup, lemon juice and remaining 4 cups of water.

To serve, pour into glasses filled with ice.

Lavender-Mint Tea Punch

2 tablespoons dried mint
1 tablespoon dried culinary lavender buds
6 cups boiling water
4 cups ginger ale
1 cup purple grape juice

Place mint and lavender in a warmed teapot. Add boiling water and steep for 10 minutes.

Strain the tea into a 3-quart pitcher and add the ginger ale and grape juice.

Chill before serving.

Lavender Hot Chocolate

Lavender adds a sweet floral flavor to this del
chocolate beverage.

2-1/2 cups milk
4 teaspoons dried culinary lavender buds
6 ounces (1 cup) semi-sweet chocolate chips

In a medium saucepan, bring milk to simmer over medium-
low heat. Remove from heat, stir in lavender, cover pan and
steep for 5 minutes. Strain milk and discard the lavender.

Add chocolate chips to warm milk and stir until melted.
Top with sweetened whipped cream if desired. Makes 4
servings.

Amaretto Lavender Peach Smoothie

When you're in the mood for something frosty and fruity, this smoothie will hit the spot.

1 (15 oz.) can of sliced peaches, drained
2 tablespoons Amaretto liqueur
1 teaspoon ground, dried culinary lavender buds
1 pint vanilla ice cream, softened

Place peaches, Amaretto and lavender in a blender and process until smooth.

Add ice cream and process until well blended. Makes 3-4 servings.

Lavender Sugar

There are two methods for making lavender sugar: a ground lavender/sugar mix and sugar infused with lavender flavor.

Ground Lavender/Sugar Mix

Place one teaspoon of ground, dried culinary lavender buds and one cup of sugar in a food processor. Process the ingredients to make a fine sugar mixture. Store in an air tight container and use for baking or sweetening beverages. This sugar makes a nice gift when presented in an attractive canister.

Infused Lavender Sugar

Mix 1 tablespoon dried culinary lavender buds with 2 cups of sugar and store in an airtight container for 3-4 weeks. Shake occasionally. Sift out the lavender buds before using the sugar in baked goods or to sweeten beverages.

Lavender Honey

1 teaspoon dried culinary lavender
1 cup honey

Place honey and lavender in a microwave safe measuring cup. Stir and heat on high power in the microwave until very warm.

Let steep about 30 minutes to infuse the lavender flavor into the honey. Strain the honey and discard the lavender.

Use on biscuits, cornbread or pancakes. Also use to sweeten your tea or in any recipe that calls for honey.

Lavender Applesauce

1 cup applesauce
1/2 teaspoon ground, dried culinary
   lavender

Grind lavender in a clean coffee grinder before measuring. Stir into applesauce until well blended.

Cover and place in refrigerator. Allow flavors to blend for several hours before using. Store flavored applesauce in the refrigerator.

Great when served with pork chops. You can also use it in cake or muffin recipes that call for applesauce.

Lavender Butter

1/2 cup (1 stick) butter or margarine,
softened
1 teaspoon ground, dried culinary
lavender

Grind lavender in a clean coffee grinder before measuring.
Stir lavender into butter.

Place butter in an airtight container in the refrigerator for
several hours to blend flavors. Store the flavored butter in
the refrigerator until ready to use.

Serve on rolls, grilled meats, cooked vegetables, or use in
baking.

Sweetened Lavender Butter

For a sweet version of lavender butter to spread on scones,
pancakes or pound cake, follow the recipe below.

1/2 cup (1 stick) unsalted butter, softened
2 tablespoons confectioner's sugar
1 teaspoon ground, dried culinary lavender buds

Grind lavender in a clean coffee grinder before measuring.
Stir sugar and lavender into butter until well blended.

Place butter in an airtight container in the refrigerator for
several hours to blend flavors. Store the flavored butter in
the refrigerator until ready to use.

Lavender Blueberry Syrup

1 teaspoon dried culinary lavender
1 cup blueberry syrup

Place lavender and syrup in microwave-safe measuring cup. Stir and heat on high power in the microwave until very warm. Let steep at about 30 minutes to blend flavors.

Strain and store in the refrigerator until ready to use. Serve on pancakes, French toast or waffles.

Lavender Extract

1 cup of 100-proof vodka (80-proof is okay, too)
1/4 cup dried culinary lavender buds

Mix the vodka and lavender together in a glass jar with a tight-fitting lid. Let them steep for one week. Strain the extract and discard the lavender.

Use the flavored vodka the same as vanilla extract to flavor cakes, cookies, puddings and whipped cream.

This recipe also makes a unique gift when presented in an attractive bottle.

Lavender Whipped Cream

1 cup heavy cream
1 tablespoon dried culinary lavender
2 tablespoons granulated sugar

Combine cream and lavender in an
airtight container. Refrigerate for 3-4
hours to allow cream to absorb the lavender flavor. Strain
cream and discard lavender.

Beat cream until soft peaks form. Add several drops of
purple food coloring (or blue and red mixed together) if
desired. Gradually add sugar and continue beating until
stiff. Serve with fresh fruit or pound cake. Makes about 2
cups.

Creamy Lavender Fruit Dip

1 (8 oz.) pkg. cream cheese, softened
1 cup sour cream
3 tablespoons granulated sugar
1 teaspoon vanilla extract
1 teaspoon ground, dried culinary
   lavender
Cut up fresh fruit of your choice

Combine all ingredients and beat until creamy. Cover and
store in the refrigerator until ready to serve. Enjoy with
fresh fruit.

Variation: Substitute almond extract for the vanilla extract
and stir in 3 tablespoons of finely chopped almonds.

Lavender "Clotted" Cream

Real clotted cream is sold in only a few specialty stores the United States or on-line, but you can make a lavender-flavored substitute using the following recipe below.

1 cup whipping cream
1 tablespoon dried culinary lavender buds
2 tablespoons confectioner's sugar
1/2 cup sour cream

Combine the cream and lavender buds in small bowl. Cover and refrigerate for 3-4 hours to allow cream to absorb the lavender flavor. Strain cream and discard lavender.

Beat the whipping cream and sugar until soft peaks form. Add a few drops of purple food coloring to the cream if desired. Gently fold in the sour cream. Chill until ready to serve. Mixture will keep up to 4 hours in the refrigerator. Serve with Lavender and Walnut Scones (recipe on page 22).

Breads
and
Pastries

Herbes de Provence Bread

1 (11 ounce) can of French bread dough (found in the
      refrigerator section in the grocery store)
2 tablespoons butter or margarine, melted
2 teaspoons Herbs de Provence (see recipe on page 37)

Preheat oven to 350°. Unroll bread dough. Brush with melted butter or margarine. Sprinkle Herbs de Provence over butter.

Re-roll dough. Place on a greased cookie sheet, seam side down. Cut diagonal slits in the top of the loaf if desired. Bake for 25-30 minutes or until golden brown.

Serve warm with Lavender Butter (page 13).

Cheesy Lavender & Garlic Biscuits

2 cups all-purpose flour
2 teaspoons baking powder
1 teaspoon ground, dried culinary
   lavender buds
1/2 teaspoon salt
1/2 cup chilled butter or margarine
1 cup grated Cheddar cheese
2/3 cup milk
1/4 cup melted butter or margarine
1/4 teaspoon garlic powder

Preheat oven to 425°.

In a large bowl, combine flour, baking powder, lavender and salt. Cut in the chilled butter with a pastry blender until mixture resembles coarse crumbs.

Stir in the cheese. Add milk and stir until dough forms a ball. Turn dough out onto a lightly floured board and knead 6 - 8 times. Roll or pat to about 3/4" thick. Cut out with a 2 to 2-1/2" biscuit cutter.

Place on a lightly greased baking sheet. Bake for 12 - 15 minutes or until golden brown.

Brush the tops of the warm biscuits with the melted butter blended with garlic powder. Makes 8-10 biscuits.

Lavender & Honey Cornbread Muffins

1-1/4 cups all-purpose flour
3/4 cup cornmeal
2 teaspoons ground, dried culinary lavender buds
1-1/2 teaspoons baking powder
1/2 teaspoon baking soda
1/2 teaspoon salt
2 eggs, slightly beaten
3/4 cup milk
1/4 cup honey
2 tablespoons butter or margarine, melted

Grind lavender in a clean coffee grinder before measuring.

Preheat the oven to 375°. Lightly grease 12 muffin cups.

In a large bowl, combine cornmeal, flour, lavender, baking powder, baking soda and salt.

In a separate bowl, combine eggs, milk, honey and butter. Stir the wet ingredients into the dry ingredients, just until moistened.

Fill muffin cups about two-thirds full. Bake 15 - 18 minutes or until golden brown. Remove the muffins from the pan and cool on a wire rack.

Lavender Blueberry Muffins

1/2 cup sugar
1/4 cup butter or margarine, softened
1 cup sour cream
2 teaspoons ground, dried culinary lavender buds
1 egg
1-1/2 cups all-purpose flour
1 teaspoon baking soda
1/4 teaspoon salt
1 cup fresh or frozen blueberries (unthawed)

Grind lavender in a coffee grinder before measuring. Preheat oven to 375°.

Beat sugar and butter in large bowl until well blended. Stir in sour cream, lavender and egg.

In a separate bowl, combine flour, baking soda and salt. Blend flour mixture into sour cream mixture just until moistened. Fold in blueberries. Spoon batter into 12 greased muffin cups.

Bake 20-25 minutes or until done. Cool 5 minutes in pan; then remove to wire rack.

Lavender Zucchini Bread

1 cup grated zucchini (about 1 large)
1 cup granulated sugar
1/2 cup vegetable oil
1 teaspoon vanilla extract
2 eggs
1-1/2 cups flour
2 teaspoons ground dried culinary lavender buds
1 teaspoon cinnamon
1/2 teaspoon salt
1/2 teaspoon baking powder
1/2 teaspoon baking soda
1/2 cup chopped pecans

Preheat oven to 350°. In a large mixing bowl, combine zucchini, sugar, oil, vanilla extract and eggs. Beat until well blended.

In a separate bowl, mix flour, lavender, cinnamon, salt, baking powder and baking soda. Stir into the zucchini mixture. Fold in pecans. Pour into a 9 x 5 x 3" greased and floured loaf pan. Bake 55-60 minutes or until done. Remove from pan and cool on wire rack.

Lemon & Lavender
Walnut Scones

2 cups flour
1/3 cup sugar
1-1/2 teaspoons baking powder
1/2 teaspoon baking soda
2 teaspoons ground, dried culinary lavender
1 teaspoon dried lemon peel
1/4 teaspoon salt
1/4 cup (4 tablespoons) unsalted butter
1 large egg, slightly beaten
1/2 cup sour cream
1 teaspoon vanilla extract
1/2 cup chopped walnuts

Grind lavender before measuring. Preheat oven to 400°. In a large bowl, combine flour, sugar, lavender, lemon peel, baking powder, baking soda and salt. Cut in butter with a pastry blender until mixture resembles coarse crumbs. In a separate bowl, mix together egg, vanilla and sour cream; stir into dry ingredients just until moistened. Stir in walnuts. Turn dough out onto a lightly floured surface; knead 8-10 times or until smooth.

Pat into a 7" circle, about 3/4" thick. Cut into 8 pie-shaped wedges. Or roll dough to 3/4" thickness and cut out circles with a 2-1/2" biscuit cutter. Brush tops with milk and sprinkle with sugar.

Place 1" apart on lightly greased cookie sheet. Bake for 15 to 18 minutes, or until golden brown. Serve warm with Lavender Infused Honey (page 12) or Lavender "Clotted" Cream (page 16).

Appetizers

Lavender Shrimp Salad

1-1/4 cups cooked shrimp, finely chopped
2/3 cup finely chopped celery
1/3 cup mayonnaise
1 tablespoon minced green onion
1 teaspoon ground, dried culinary lavender buds
Salt and pepper to taste

Combine shrimp, celery and onion in a medium bowl. Add mayonnaise, lavender, salt and pepper. Lightly mix until well blended.

Cover and chill for 2 hours to blend flavors.

Serve with your favorite crackers.

-OR- Slice one cucumber into 1/8" slices. Top each slice with shrimp salad. Cover and refrigerate until ready to serve. Makes about 20 appetizers.

Lavender & Cream Cheese Cucumber Sandwiches

1 (8-ounce package) cream cheese, softened
1 teaspoon ground, dried culinary lavender buds
1 cucumber, peeled and thinly sliced
Salt and pepper to taste
16 slices of whole wheat or white bread
Butter or margarine, softened

Lightly butter one side of each slice of bread.

In a small bowl, blend cream cheese and lavender. Spread 2 tablespoons of cream cheese mixture on 8 of the bread slices.

Arrange a layer of cucumber slices on top of the cream cheese. Sprinkle with salt and pepper and top with the remaining buttered bread slices. Trim away crusts and cut into 4 triangles.

Cover and refrigerate until ready to serve. Makes 32.

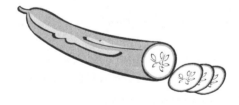

Lavender, Ham & Pineapple Pinwheels

1/2 cup cream cheese, softened
1/4 cup ground, smoked ham
1/4 cup crushed pineapple, well drained
1 teaspoon ground, dried culinary lavender buds
8 slices of soft, white or whole wheat bread

In a small mixing bowl, blend together the cream cheese, ham, pineapple and lavender. Trim crusts off bread and flatten bread slices slightly with a rolling pin or fingers.

Spread 2 tablespoons of filling onto each slice of bread. Roll up jelly-roll fashion and wrap in plastic wrap. Chill at least 2 hours or until firm enough to slice.

Remove plastic wrap and slice each roll into 5 pieces (3/4" slices). Recipe makes 40 pinwheels.

Mini Lavender & Zucchini Quiches

2 large eggs
1/2 cup half-and-half
1 teaspoon ground, dried culinary lavender buds
1/4 teaspoon onion powder
1/4 teaspoon salt
Dash of pepper
1/2 cup shredded Swiss cheese
1/2 cup shredded zucchini
1 (15 ounce) package of refrigerated pastry dough
        (2 crusts for 9" pie)

Preheat oven to 350°. Unroll pastry dough and cut into 24 circles using a 3" biscuit cutter. Line mini muffin cups with dough.

Place about 1 teaspoon zucchini into each muffin cup.

In a measuring cup with a pouring spout, beat eggs, half-and-half, lavender, onion powder, salt and pepper. Fill muffin cups 3/4 full with egg mixture.

Sprinkle about one teaspoon of cheese on top of each quiche.

Bake 20-25 minutes until pastry is golden brown and centers are set. Let stand 10 minutes before removing from pan.

Cool on wire rack. Serve warm or cold.

Stuffed Cherry Tomatoes with Lavender

24 cherry tomatoes
6 ounces cream cheese, softened
1/2 teaspoon ground, dried culinary lavender buds
Dash of salt

Cut tops from tomatoes and scoop out insides. Drain upside down on a paper towels.

In a small bowl, beat cream cheese, lavender and salt together. Fill each tomato shell with cream cheese mixture. Refrigerate until ready to serve.

Lavender Stuffed Eggs

12 hard-boiled eggs
1/3 cup finely chopped celery
1 tablespoon minced onion
1/3 cup mayonnaise
1 teaspoon mustard
1 teaspoon ground, dried culinary lavender buds
1/4 teaspoon salt

Peel eggs and cut in half lengthwise. Remove and mash egg yolks. Finely dice 1 whole egg white.

In medium bowl, combine yolks, diced egg white, celery, onion, mayonnaise, mustard, lavender and salt. Spoon about 1 tablespoon filling into each egg white half. Cover and refrigerate until ready to serve.

Lavender Chicken Salad Puffs

1 package (17.3 oz.) frozen puff pastry, thawed
2 cups chopped cooked chicken
2/3 cup finely chopped celery
2 tablespoons finely chopped green onion
2 teaspoons ground, dried culinary lavender buds
2/3 cup mayonnaise
1/4 cup chopped, toasted almonds*
Salt and pepper to taste

In a medium bowl, combine chicken, celery, green onion, lavender, mayonnaise, almonds, salt and pepper. Mix until well blended. Chill for several hours to blend flavors.

To prepare puffs, preheat oven to 400°. Unroll pastry dough onto lightly floured surface. Cut puff pastry into assorted shapes (hearts, diamonds, circles) using 2-1/2" cookie or biscuit cutters. Place 1" apart on ungreased baking sheet. Bake for 12 - 15 minutes or until puffed and golden. Cool on wire racks.

Cut puffs in half, horizontally. Spoon about 2 teaspoons of chicken mixture into puffs and replace tops. Makes about 32 puffs.

*Toast almonds in a dry skillet over medium heat, stirring frequently until golden brown. Cool before adding to chicken salad mixture.

Soups & Stews

Pork & Hominy Stew with Lavender

4 slices smoked bacon
1-1/2 pounds lean pork cut into 1/2" cubes
1/2 cup chopped onion
2 (14 ounce) cans chicken broth
2 (15.5 ounce) cans of white hominy, drained
1 (4 ounce) can mild, diced green chilies, drained
2 teaspoons ground, dried culinary lavender
1/2 teaspoon garlic powder
Salt and pepper to taste

In a Dutch oven, fry bacon until crisp. Remove from pan and set aside to drain. Add pork to bacon drippings in Dutch oven and cook until browned. Stir in onion and cook until tender.

Add hominy, broth, bacon (crumbled), green chilies, lavender and garlic powder. Cover and simmer about one hour or until meat is tender, stirring occasionally.

White Chili with Lavender

1/2 cup chopped onion
1 tablespoon vegetable oil
2 (14 ounce) cans chicken broth
2-1/2 cups chopped, cooked chicken
2 (15-1/2 oz.) cans great northern beans, drained and rinsed
1 (4 ounce) can mild, diced green chilies, drained
2 teaspoons ground, dried culinary lavender
1/2 teaspoon garlic powder
2 tablespoons cornstarch
Salt and pepper to taste

In a Dutch oven, sauté onion in oil until tender. Stir in broth, beans, chicken, green chilies, lavender and garlic powder. Bring to a boil over medium high heat.

Combine cornstarch with 1/4 cup water and add to chili. Cook over medium heat, stirring frequently, until thickened. Makes 4-5 servings.

Serve with Lavender and Honey Cornbread Muffins on page 19.

Lavender Corn Chowder

2 cups peeled and chopped potato
1 cup chopped celery
1/3 cup chopped onion
1 tablespoon vegetable oil
2 cups water
1 cup half & half
2 (14-3/4 ounce) cans cream style corn
6 slices smoked bacon, cooked and crumbled
2 teaspoons ground, dried culinary lavender buds
1/2 teaspoon garlic powder
Salt & pepper to taste

In a large saucepan, sauté celery and onion in vegetable oil until tender. Add the potato and water. Cover and simmer 20 minutes or until potato is tender. Stir in corn, half & half, bacon and seasonings. Heat through but do not boil. Makes about 4-5 servings.

Lavender & Broccoli Cheese Soup

3 tablespoons butter or margarine
2 tablespoons finely chopped onion
3 tablespoons flour
2 teaspoons chicken bouillon granules
1 teaspoon ground, dried culinary lavender buds
1/2 teaspoon garlic powder
1/4 teaspoon salt
1/8 teaspoon pepper
1 cup water
2 cups milk
2 cups shredded cheddar cheese
1 cup cooked, chopped broccoli florets

In a large saucepan, cook onions in butter until tender. Stir in flour and cook one minute. Add seasonings and water. Cook over medium heat, stirring constantly until thick. Stir in milk and cheese and cook until cheese is melted. Add broccoli and heat through. Makes 4 servings.

Salads

Lavender Melon Salad

1/2 cup water
1/3 cup granulated sugar
1 tablespoon lemon juice
1 teaspoon ground, dried culinary lavender buds
1-1/2 cups cantaloupe, cubed
1-1/2 cups honey dew melon, cubed
2 cups watermelon, cubed
1/2 cup fresh blueberries

Combine water, sugar, lemon juice and lavender in a saucepan. Bring to a boil, stirring constantly for about 5 minutes. Remove from heat, cover and chill.

In a large bowl, combine fruit. Pour syrup over fruit and stir to coat. Cover and store in the refrigerator several hours to blend flavors. Drain before serving.

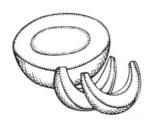

Lavender & Green Pea Salad

This crunchy, cool salad is perfect for an outdoor summer picnic.

2-1/2 cups frozen peas, thawed & drained
1/2 cup sour cream
1/2 cup chopped red bell pepper
2 tablespoons green onions, chopped
1 teaspoon ground, dried culinary lavender buds
5 slices of smoked bacon, cooked and crumbled
Salt and pepper to taste

In a medium bowl, combine peas, sour cream, bell pepper, lavender and onion. Chill for several hours to blend flavors. Stir in bacon just before serving. Makes about 6 servings.

Creamy Lavender Pineapple Salad

1 cup miniature marshmallows
1 pkg. (4-serving size) pistachio flavor instant pudding
2 teaspoons ground, dried culinary lavender
1 can (20 oz.) crushed pineapple, in juice, undrained
1/2 cup chopped pecans
1-1/2 cups frozen whipped topping, thawed

Combine marshmallows, dry pudding mix, lavender, pineapple and pecans in a large bowl until well blended. Add whipped topping. Stir gently until well blended. Cover and refrigerate at least 1 hour before serving.

Lavender & Thyme Salad Dressing

3 tablespoons lemon juice
1/2 cup vegetable oil
1 teaspoon ground, dried culinary lavender
1 teaspoon dried thyme leaves, crushed
1/2 teaspoon ground, dry mustard
1/2 teaspoon salt
1/2 teaspoon onion powder
1/4 teaspoon garlic powder
1/4 teaspoon ground black pepper

Combine all ingredients in a small jar with a tight fitting lid. Shake well to blend. Refrigerate for several hours to blend flavors. Store in refrigerator until ready to use.

Shake well before serving. Drizzle over mixture of salad greens and salad veggies of your choice.

Ham & Apricot Pasta Salad with Lavender

2 cups uncooked spiral pasta
3/4 cup sour cream
1/2 cup mayonnaise
1 teaspoon ground, dried culinary lavender buds
Salt & black pepper to taste
1/2 cup diced celery
1/2 cup dried apricots, chopped
1/4 cup finely chopped green onions
1/2 pound smoked ham, cut into thin strips
1/2 pound Swiss cheese cut into thin strips

Cook pasta according to package directions. Rinse with cold water. Drain and set aside.

In a small bowl, combine sour cream, mayonnaise, lavender, salt and black pepper. Combine remaining ingredients in a large bowl. Stir in sour cream mixture. Add cooked pasta and toss to coat.

Cover and refrigerate at least 1 hour. Makes 4-5 servings.

Main Dishes & Sides

Several of the following recipes include an herb blend called Herbs de Provence. There are many recipes for Herbs de Provence and you can mix one according to your own preference.

Experiment with various proportions of the following herbs to find the flavor blend you like best. All the herbs are crushed or ground.

Herbs De Provence

1 tablespoon dried oregano leaves
1 tablespoon dried thyme leaves
1 tablespoon dried culinary lavender buds
1 teaspoon dried basil leaves
1 teaspoon dried sage leaves
1 teaspoon dried rosemary leaves

Grind lavender buds in a clean coffee grinder. Finely chop or crush remaining spices. Combine all ingredients and blend well. Store in an airtight container in a cool, dark place.

Lavender Mashed Potatoes

4 large Russet potatoes, peeled & cubed
2/3 cup half-and-half
4 tablespoons butter
2 teaspoons Herbs de Provence
Salt and pepper to taste

Place the potatoes in a large sauce pan. Cover with water and bring to a boil. Cover and cook for 20-25 minutes or until tender.

In a small saucepan, heat half-and-half until very hot but not boiling. Add butter and herbs de Provence. Keep warm. Drain and mash the potatoes. Add the milk mixture, then beat until fluffy. Add salt and pepper. Makes 4 servings.

Lavender Roasted Tomatoes

6 medium tomatoes, quartered
2 teaspoons Herbs de Provence
2 tablespoons olive oil
Salt and pepper to taste

Preheat oven to 300°.

In a medium bowl, toss tomatoes with herbs, oil, salt and pepper. Place in a single layer in a shallow baking pan, cut side up.

Roast for about 2 hours or until soft. Serve as a side dish or toss with pasta or use on sandwiches.

Lavender Vegetable Medley

1/3 cup butter or margarine
1 cup peeled, cubed potatoes
1 cup frozen corn kernels
1/2 cup diced carrots
1/3 cup chopped onion
1/2 cup chopped, canned tomatoes
1 teaspoon ground, dried culinary lavender buds
1/2 teaspoon sugar
Salt & pepper to taste

In a medium saucepan, melt butter. Add remaining ingredients. Cover and cook over medium low heat, stirring occasionally for about 20 minutes or until vegetables are tender.

Lavender Rice Pilaf

1 tablespoon vegetable oil
1 cup long-grain rice, uncooked
1/2 cup onion, chopped
3 teaspoons chicken bouillon granules
1 teaspoon ground, dried culinary lavender buds
1 teaspoon dried basil leaves, crushed
Dash of black pepper
2 cups water

Heat oil in a saucepan over medium-high heat. Add rice and cook until light brown. Stir in onion and cook until tender. Add bouillon, lavender, basil, pepper and water. Bring to a boil, cover and simmer over low heat 20 minutes or until water is absorbed.

Chicken and Lavender Pizza

One 12", pre-baked pizza shell
8 ounces (2 cups) grated mozzarella cheese
1-1/2 cups chopped, cooked chicken
1/4 cup chopped onion
1 tablespoon olive oil
2 teaspoons Herbs de Provence

Preheat oven to 450°. In a small skillet, sauté onion in oil until tender. Spread onion and oil on pizza shell. Sprinkle chicken on top, followed by the herbs and cheese. Bake 10 minutes, or until cheese is melted and bubbling.

For variation: Place several very thin slices of tomato over onion before adding chicken. Top with herbs and cheese.

-OR- Add 1 cup of chopped, cooked potato before adding the chicken. Top with herbs and cheese.

Lavender Dry Rub for Steaks

Use this dry rub on chicken and pork, as well as beef.

2 teaspoons ground, dried culinary lavender buds
1 teaspoon garlic powder
1 teaspoon onion powder
1 teaspoon paprika
1 teaspoon dried lemon peel
1/2 teaspoon salt
1/4 teaspoon black pepper

Blend all ingredients together and store in an air-tight container. Rub a generous amount of dry rub mixture onto both sides of steaks and let stand in the refrigerator several hours before grilling. Grill to desired doneness.

Lavender & Shrimp Stuffed Potatoes

4 large Idaho potatoes, baked
5 tablespoons butter, divided
2 cups grated cheddar cheese (reserve 1/4 cup for topping)
1 cup sour cream
1 teaspoon Herbs de Provence
Salt and pepper to taste
1 pound medium size shrimp, peeled and de-veined
Paprika

Preheat oven to 350°.

Cook shrimp in a large skillet in 1 tablespoon of the butter over medium high heat until pink (about 3-4 minutes). Drain and set aside.

Place the remaining 4 tablespoons of butter in a large bowl. Slice each potato in half lengthwise. Gently scoop out the warm potato and place in the bowl. Using an electric mixer, beat the potatoes, butter, sour cream, Herbs de Provence, salt and pepper until fluffy.

Fold the shrimp and cheese into the potatoes. Fill the potato shells with the mixture. Top each potato with 1 tablespoon reserved grated cheese and sprinkle lightly with paprika.

Place potatoes on a baking sheet and bake in the oven for 20 to 25 minutes, until heated through and lightly browned on top.

Chicken & Pasta Alfredo with Lavender

3 cups uncooked penne pasta
3 tablespoons butter
1 large red bell pepper, cut into thin strips
2/3 cup chopped onion
3 cups chopped, cooked chicken
2 teaspoons ground, dried culinary lavender buds
1 teaspoon dried basil leaves, crushed
1/2 teaspoon garlic powder
1 cup heavy cream
1/2 cup grated Parmesan cheese
Salt and pepper to taste

Cook pasta according to package directions. Drain and set aside.

Grind lavender in a clean coffee grinder before measuring. Melt butter in a large skillet. Add bell pepper and onion and sauté until vegetables are tender.

Add chicken, lavender, basil, garlic powder and cream. Simmer for a few minutes to thicken sauce.

Stir in cheese. Add pasta and toss to coat. Serve with extra grated Parmesan cheese. Makes 4 servings.

Creamy Lavender Baked Salmon

2 pounds salmon fillets
1 cup sour cream
2 tablespoons lemon juice
2 teaspoons ground, dried culinary lavender buds
1/2 teaspoon garlic powder
Salt and pepper to taste

Preheat oven to 400°. Rinse salmon fillets and pat dry. Place in a single layer, skin side down in a lightly greased 9"x13" baking pan.

In a small bowl, blend sour cream, lemon juice, lavender and garlic powder. Spread sauce over salmon. Sprinkle with salt and pepper. Bake 15 – 20 minutes or until flaky.

Lavender & Apple Pork Tenderloin

1 to 1 1/2 pounds pork tenderloin
2 tablespoons cornstarch
1 teaspoon ground cinnamon
1 teaspoon ground, dried culinary lavender
1/2 teaspoon dried, grated lemon peel
2 tablespoons brown sugar, packed
2 large apples, peeled and chopped
2 tablespoons dried cranberries, chopped (optional)

Preheat oven to 400°. Place tenderloin in a baking pan or casserole dish. Combine remaining ingredients in a bowl. Spoon the apple mixture around the tenderloin.

Cover and bake 35 minutes. Remove lid and spoon apple mixture over tenderloin. Recover and continue baking for about 20 minutes or until pork is done. Makes 4 servings.

Lavender Roasted Chicken

4 boneless, skinless chicken breasts (about 1-1/2 lbs.)
1/4 cup butter or margarine, melted
1 teaspoon ground, dried culinary lavender buds
1/2 teaspoon dried parsley flakes
1/2 teaspoon ground, dried sage
1/4 teaspoon onion powder
Salt and pepper to taste

Grind lavender in a clean coffee grinder before measuring. Preheat oven to 350°. Rinse chicken breasts and pat dry. Place in a shallow, lightly greased baking dish.

In a small bowl, combine butter, lavender, parsley, sage, and onion powder. Spoon butter mixture over the chicken. Sprinkle with salt and pepper. Bake 35-40 minutes or until done.

Desserts

Lavender Chocolate Fudge

2 cups (one 12-oz. pkg.) semi-sweet chocolate chips
1 (14 oz.) can sweetened condensed milk
2 teaspoons ground, dried culinary lavender buds
Dash of salt
1/2 cup chopped pecans
1 teaspoon vanilla extract

Grind lavender in a clean coffee grinder before measuring.

In a small, microwave-safe bowl, heat chocolate chips, condensed milk and salt together in the microwave on high power for 1 minute. Stir and then heat an additional 30 seconds if needed. Do not allow to boil. Stir until smooth and all chips are melted.

Stir in lavender, pecans and vanilla. Pour into an 8" square pan lined with foil. Chill until firm then cut into 1" squares.

Lavender Tea Cookies

1/2 cup sugar
1/4 cup butter or margarine
1 large egg
2 teaspoons ground, dried culinary lavender buds
1/4 teaspoon dried lemon peel
1 cup flour
1 teaspoon baking powder
1/8 teaspoon salt

Grind lavender in a clean coffee grinder or food processor before measuring. Preheat oven to 375°.

Cream together butter and sugar. Add egg, lavender and lemon peel; mix well.

In a separate bowl, blend the flour, baking powder and salt. Add the dry ingredients to the creamed mixture and mix well. Drop by teaspoonfuls onto lightly greased cookie sheet.

Bake about 12 - 14 minutes. Don't over-brown. Remove from oven and cool on wire racks. Makes about 18 cookies. Serve with Relaxing Lavender Tea (page 5).

Lemon and Lavender
Pound Cake

1 tablespoon lemon juice
1/2 tablespoon fresh, grated lemon peel
1/2 cup milk
1-1/2 cups all-purpose flour
1/4 teaspoon salt
1/4 teaspoon baking soda
1/4 teaspoon baking powder
2 teaspoons ground, dried culinary lavender
1/2 cup butter, softened
3/4 cup sugar
2 large eggs

Glaze:
1/3 cup powdered sugar
1 tablespoon lemon juice

Preheat oven to 350°. Grease and flour a 9" loaf pan.

In a measuring cup, blend milk, lemon juice and lemon peel; set aside. In a small bowl, blend flour, salt, soda, baking powder and lavender.

In a medium mixing bowl, cream butter and sugar together. Add eggs and beat until mixture is fluffy. Gradually add flour mixture alternately with the milk mixture. Pour batter into prepared pan. Bake for 40 to 45 minutes, or until done. Remove from the oven and let cool 5 minutes before removing from pan. Place cake on a wire rack to cool.

To prepare glaze: Stir together powdered sugar and lemon juice. Brush glaze on top of warm cake.

Mini Lavender Cheesecakes

Crust:
1 cup graham cracker crumbs
3 tablespoons sugar
3 tablespoons butter or margarine, melted

Filling:
2 (8-ounce) packages cream cheese, softened
3/4 cup sugar
2 eggs
2 teaspoons ground, dried culinary lavender buds
1 teaspoon vanilla extract

Preheat oven to 350°. Line 18 muffin cups with paper liners.

Mix crust ingredients together and press about 1 tablespoon of mixture into bottom of each cup.

Beat cream cheese until fluffy. Add sugar, eggs, lavender and vanilla extract, blending well.

Spoon cream cheese mixture into muffin cups. Bake for 15 - 20 minutes or until set.

Cool before removing from pans. Chill until ready to serve.

Lavender Chocolate Brownies

1/2 cup butter or margarine, melted
1 cup granulated sugar
2 large eggs
1 teaspoon vanilla extract
3/4 cup all-purpose flour
1/3 cup unsweetened cocoa powder
1-1/2 teaspoons ground, dried culinary
    lavender
1/4 teaspoon baking powder
1/8 teaspoon salt
1/2 cup chopped pecans
1/2 cup semi-sweet chocolate chips

Grind lavender in a clean coffee grinder before measuring. Preheat oven to 350°.

In a medium bowl, mix butter, sugar, eggs and vanilla until well blended.

In a separate bowl, blend together flour, cocoa, lavender, baking powder and salt. Stir flour mixture into egg mixture. Add pecans and chocolate chips.

Pour batter into a lightly greased 8" square baking pan. Bake 35-40 minutes or until done. Cool completely before cutting into squares.

Lavender Fruit Shells

1 package frozen puff pastry shells (6)
1 package (about 3.5 oz.) vanilla
    instant pudding mix
2 cups milk
2 tablespoons dried culinary lavender
2 cups cut-up fresh fruit (strawberries,
    grapes, peaches, blueberries, etc.)
Frozen whipped topping, thawed

Combine the milk and lavender buds in small bowl. Cover and refrigerate for 3-4 hours to allow milk to absorb the lavender flavor. Strain milk and discard lavender.

Bake pastry shells according to package directions. Remove from baking sheet and cool completely on a wire rack.

Prepare pudding using lavender infused milk. Mix according to package directions.

Spoon about 1/3 cup of pudding into each pastry shell. Top with fruit. Serve with whipped topping.

Serve immediately or cover and refrigerate up to 4 hours. Makes 6 servings.

Lavender & Cinnamon Apple Cake

1 cup granulated sugar
1/2 cup vegetable oil
1 teaspoon vanilla extract
2 large eggs, slightly beaten
1-1/2 cups peeled and chopped apples
1-1/2 cups all-purpose flour
2 teaspoons ground, dried culinary lavender buds
1 teaspoon ground cinnamon
1/2 teaspoon baking soda
1/4 teaspoon salt
1/2 cup chopped pecans

Grind lavender in a clean coffee grinder before measuring. Preheat oven to 350°. In a large bowl, blend sugar, oil, vanilla and eggs. Stir in apples.

In a separate bowl, mix together flour, salt, baking soda, lavender and cinnamon. Add to egg mixture, stirring until well blended. Stir in pecans.

Pour into a greased and floured 8" square baking pan. Bake for 35-40 minutes or until done.

Cool completely in pan. Cut into squares and serve topped with Lavender Whipped Cream (page 15) if desired.

A Taste of Lavender

Lavender is a beautiful, fragrant and tasty herb that has a wide range of culinary uses. *A Taste of Lavender* includes just a small sampling of the many possibilities.

Delight your family and dinner guests by adding the deliciously distinctive flavor of lavender to your cooking.

Experiment with the recipes offered in this book to spark your creativity and tickle your taste buds.

Index

Chicken Pizza, 40
Dry Rub for Steaks, 40
Herbes de Provence, 37
Pork Tenderloin, 43
Potatoes (Mashed), 38
Rice Pilaf, 39
Salmon (Baked), 43
Shrimp Stuffed Potatoes,
41
Tomatoes (Roasted), 38
Vegetable Medley, 39

Desserts:

Apple Cake, 51
Brownies, 49
Cheesecakes (Mini), 48
Fudge (Chocolate), 45
Fruit Shells, 50
Lemon Pound Cake, 47
Tea Cookies, 46

Ordering Information for Dried Culinary Lavender

Below is a list of companies that sell dried culinary lavender online. You can locate others simply by typing "dried culinary lavender" into your computer search engine.

- San Francisco Herb Co: www.sfherb.com
- Mountain Rose Herbs:
  www.mountainroseherbs.com
- Bulk Foods: www.bulkfoods.com

About the Author

Gloria Hander Lyons has channeled 30 years of training and hands-on experience in the areas of art, interior decorating, crafting and event planning into writing creative how-to books. Her books cover a wide range of topics including decorating your home, cooking, planning weddings and tea parties, crafting and self-publishing.

Gloria has designed original craft projects featured in magazines, such as *Better Homes and Gardens, McCall's, Country Handcrafts* and *Crafts*. She teaches interior decorating, event planning and self-publishing classes at her local community college. Much to her family's delight, her kitchen is in non-stop test mode, creating recipes for new cookbooks.

Visit her website: www.BlueSagePress.com

Other Books by Gloria Hander Lyons:
- *Easy Microwave Desserts in a Mug*
- *Easy Microwave Desserts in a Mug for Kids*
- *No Rules – Just Fun Decorating*
- *Just Fun Decorating for Tweens & Teens*
- *Decorating Basics: For Men Only*
- *If Teapots Could Talk—Fun Ideas for Tea Parties*
- *The Super-Bride's Guide for Dodging Wedding Pitfalls*
- *Lavender Sensations: Fragrant Herbs for Home & Bath*
- *Designs That Sell: How to Make Your Home Show Better & Sell Faster*
- *Self-Publishing on a Budget: A Do-It-All-Yourself Guide*
- *The Secret Ingredient: Tasty Recipes with an Unusual Twist*
- *Hand Over the Chocolate & No One Gets Hurt: The Chocolate-Lover's Cookbook*

Ordering Information

To order additional copies of this book, send check or money order payable to:

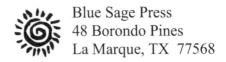 Blue Sage Press
48 Borondo Pines
La Marque, TX 77568

Cost for this edition is $6.95 per book (U.S. currency only) plus $3.00 shipping and handling for the first book and $1.25 for each additional book shipped to the same U.S. address.

Texas residents add 8.25% sales tax to total order amount.

To pay by credit card or get a complete list of books written by Gloria Hander Lyons, visit our website:

www.BlueSagePress.com

CPSIA information can be obtained
at www.ICGtesting.com
Printed in the USA
LVOW04s1834130816
500262LV00033B/650/P